SPORTS SOCIOLOGY IN PHYSICAL EDUCATION

DR. A. SAKTHIVEL

Copyright © Dr. A. Sakthivel
All Rights Reserved.

Dedicated to My beloved Father Mr. A. Arunagiri

my mother Mrs. A. Valliammal

Contents

● v ●

I
SPORTS SOCIOLOGY

The study of the development, structure, and functioning of human society.

ORIGIN

Mid 19th century: from French sociology (see socio, -logy). Translate sociology to Use over time for sociology.

DEFINITION OF SPORTS SOCIOLOGY

Sociology of sport alternately referred to as sports sociology, is a sub-discipline of sociology that focuses on sports as social phenomena. It is an area of study concerned with the relationship between sociology and sports, and also various socio-cultural structures, patterns, and organizations or groups involved with the sport. This area of the study discusses the positive impact sports have on individual people and society as a whole economically, financially, and socially. Sociology of sport attempts to view the actions and behavior of sports teams and their players through the eyes of a sociologist.

Sports Sociology is the study of social behavior or society, including its origins, development, organization, networks, and institutions. It is a social science that uses various methods of empirical investigation and critical analysis to develop a body of knowledge about social order, disorder, and change.

MEANING OF SPORTS SOCIOLOGY

Sports Sociology is the study of social behavior or society including its origins, development, organization, networks institutions. It is a social science that uses various methods of empirical investigation and critical analysis to develop a body of knowledge about social order, disorder, and change. Many sociologists aim to conduct research that may be applied directly to social policy and welfare, while others focus primarily on refining the theoretical understanding of social processes.

Subject matter ranges from the micro Sociology of individual agency and interaction to the macro level of systems and the social structure.

The traditional focuses of sociology include social stratification, social class, social mobility, religion, secularization, law, sexuality, and deviance. As all spheres of human activity are affected by the interplay between social structure and individual agency, sociology has gradually expanded its focus to further subjects, such as health, medical, military, and penal institutions, the internet, education, economic status the role of social activity in the development of scientific knowledge.

The range of social scientific methods has also expanded. social researchers draw upon a variety of qualitative and quantitative techniques. The linguistic and cultural turn of the mid-twentieth century led to increasingly interpretative, hermeneutic, philosophic approaches towards the analysis of society. Conversely, the end of the 1990s and the beginning of the 2000s have seen the rise of new analytically, mathematically, and computationally rigorous techniques, such as agent-based modelingand social network analysis, socialnetwork. social research policymakers, politicians, educators, planners, legislators, administrators, developers, business magnates, social workers, non-governmental organizations, non -profit. Organizations, and people interested in resolving social issues in general. There is often a great deal of crossover between social research, market research, and other statistical fields.

Sport and Games Needs and Importance of Sociology

Organized sport has the power of its global popularity, political resonance, and economic weight. But sports organizations can lose social and ethical perspective because, in an intensely competitive and increasingly lucrative global sport and ancillary industry environment, they are often subject to 'tunnel vision'. By this, I mean that there is an over-concentration on competitive advantage in relation to other sports and/or sports organizations, and a diminishing concern with the maintenance and development of a wide-ranging and positive relationship between sports and the societies that nurture them. Sport is also prone to excessive myth-making that seeks to place it beyond the everyday world of politics and material struggle. Yet, paradoxically, sport is often – sometimes cynically, sometimes sentimentally – the plaything of the political apparatus. Critical sociology is an essential corrective to this tendency, its organized skepticism constantly asking troubling questions about who wins and who loses – and that does not only mean on the sporting field.

Sociology, therefore, should be dedicated in part to saving sport from itself. This does not mean that sociologists always have the right answers, but they can puncture some of the sport's most egregious pretensions and mystifications. In this task, they need to engage not only with sportspeople and organizations, but governments, corporations, fans, and the citizenry at large. Sociologists can bring to bear theoretical explanation and empirical research that spans space (from global to transnational to national to local), time (from pre-modern to modern to postmodern), and social location (from the domestic hearth to major institutions, from primary groups to mass audiences).

There is no shortage of subjects for this engaged intellectual work. Examples include:

- The governance of sports organizations
- The priorities behind the allocation of state and private funding to sport
- Sport's environmental impact and contribution to urban inequality, especially via mega-events
- The effect of professionalization and commercialization on sport and its communities
- The enlistment of sport in social classification and hierarchy, notably class, 'race'/ethnicity, sex/gender, and sexuality
- The uses of sport as ideological metaphor and smokescreen
- The media's role in 'framing' sport and 'petrifying' culture

- The exploitation of sport by gambling and other unhealthy industries, such as fast food and alcohol
- The exploitation by the sport of vulnerable people, including aspirant and actual sports workers, and fans
- Hyper-competitiveness in sport and socially deleterious attitudes and behavior, and a corresponding diminution of its pleasurable and playful dimensions

- Sport's role in the making and unmaking of cultural citizens, and in social inclusion and exclusion.

Sport, then, needs sociology to be insistent in researching and raising these matters because, when there are inevitable and recurrent crises and problems, sports and those who fund, regulate, and monitor them often have little idea of how to prevent or manage such discomfiting matters. Too often there is a facile and routine resort to public relations, scandal management, banal reaffirmation, or projection of responsibility onto the wider society. Sociology can help guide sports organizations and policymakers in eschewing the superficial preoccupation with effect and neglect of cause that inevitably inhibits its development as a progressive social institution. In this task, it can function as a constructively critical friend rather than as a sideline adversary.

Socialization

Is a term used by sociologists, social psychologists, anthropologists, political scientists, and educationalists to refer to the lifelong process of inheriting and disseminating norms, customs, values, and ideologies, providing an individual with the skills and habits necessary for participating within their own society socialization is thus "the means by which social and cultural continuity are attained"

Socialization describes a process that may lead to desirable outcomes sometimes labeled "moral"—as regards the society where it occurs. Individual views on certain issues, for instance, race or economics, are influenced by the society's consensus and usually tend toward what that society finds acceptable or "normal". Many socio-political theories postulate that socialization provides only a partial explanation for human beliefs and behaviors, maintaining that agents are not blank slates predetermined by their environment; scientific research provides evidence that people are shaped by both social influences and genes. Genetic studies have shown that a person's environment interacts with his or her genotype to influence behavioral outcomes.

Types of Socialization

- Primary socialization. This type of socialization happens when a child learns the values, norms, and behaviors that should be displayed in order to live accordingly to a specific culture. ...
- Secondary socialization.
- Developmental socialization.
- Anticipatory socialization.
- Resocialization

Definition and types of socialization Socialization:
Man is not only social but also cultural. It is the culture that provides opportunities for men to develop their personalities. The

development of personality is not an automatic process. Every society prescribes its own ways and means of giving social training to its newborn member so that they may develop their own personality. This social training is called socialization.

The human child comes into the world as a biological organism with animal needs. He gradually molded-in society into a social being and learns a social way of acting and feeling.

The process of molding and shaping the personality of the human infant is called socialization. Some definition is to be given below that help to better understand socialization.

W.F.Ogburn: "Socialization is the process by which the individual learns to conform to the norms of the group."

Bogardus: "Socialization is the process of working together, of developing group responsibility, or being guided by the welfare needs of others."

Peter Worsley explains socialization as the process of Transmission of culture, the process whereby men learn the rules and practices of social groups.

Finally, we can say that the process of adjustment in a social environment is called socialization.

Types of socialization:

David and Jary told some types of socialization: 1. Primary socialization:

This is the most essential and basic type of socialization. It takes place in the early years of the life of the newborn individual. It concentrates on the teaching of language and cognitive skills, the interaction of culture, norms, and values, the establishment of emotional ties, and the appreciation of other roles and perspectives. The human child does not have a sense of right and wrong, desirable and undesirable, moral and immoral. By trial and error by direct and indirect observation and experience, the child gradually learns the norms relating to right and wrong behavior. Process whereby people learn the language, attitude, values, and action.

- Development socialization:
- This kind of learning is based on the achievements of primary socialization. "It builds on already acquired skills and knowledge as the adult progress through new situations such as marriage or new jobs. These new expectations, obligations, and roles. New learning is added to and blended with old in a relatively smooth and continuous process of development"—Ian Robertson.

    Anticipatory socialization:
- Men not only learn the culture of the group of which they are immediate members. They may also learn the culture of groups to which they do not belong. A person who intends to join the army may start doing physical exercises to toughen his body and learn the manners of the army. Socialization is not a process that takes place merely in early childhood. On the other hand, it takes at different times and places throughout life.
- Re socialization:
- It does not only do individuals change roles within groups, but they also change membership – groups. It may also happen in periods of rapid social mobility. For example, a newly wedded housewife may be forced to become a prostitute in a brother. In this instance, the social role of the individual got changed radically.

1. Broad socialization:

It is intended to promote independence, individualism, and self-expression. Exam: schoolboy or collage boy doesn't have more independence than a university student.

2. Narrow socialization:

It is intended to promote obedient and conformity.

Exam: you have to clean your table.

3. Natural socialization:

Occurs when infants and young starts explore, play and discover the social word. Exam: natural process when they play the action as bride or bridegroom. "The human infants learn Russo from nature."

4. Planed socialization:

Occurs when other people take action desire to teach or train others from infancy. Exam: an elder brother can teach his younger's how to respect other.

5. Positive socialization:

Positive socialization is the social learning that is best on pleasure existing experience.

6. Negative socialization:

Negative socialization occurred when others use punishment.

TYPES OF GROUP

Social Groups and Organization. A social group is two or more humans who interact with one another, share similar characteristics, and collectively have a sense of unity. A primary group is typically a small social group whose members share close, personal, enduring relationships.

Types of Social Groups: Primary, Secondary and Reference Groups

The study of social groups is a main focus of many sociologists. In this lesson, we define social groups and differentiate between several different types including primary, secondary, and reference groups.

1. Social Groups

Social groups are everywhere and are a basic part of human life; everywhere you look there seems to be groups of people! A main focus of sociology is the study of these social groups. A **social group** consists of two or more people who regularly interact and share a sense of unity and common identity. In other words, it's a group of people who see each other frequently and consider themselves a part of the group. Except in rare cases, we all typically belong to many different types of social groups. For example, you could be a member of a sports team, club, church group, college class, workplace, and more.

Primary Groups

No two groups are created equal. Each typically has its own purpose, culture, norms, etc. Sociologists differentiate between several different types of social groups. In this lesson, we'll discuss primary groups, secondary groups, and reference groups. Primary groupsare those that are close-knit. They are typically small scale, include intimate relationships, and are usually long-lasting. The members of primary groups feel a strong personal identity with the group.

Secondary Groups

Secondary groups are another type of social group. They have the opposite characteristics of primary groups. They can be small or large and are mostly impersonal and usually short term. These groups are typically found at work and school. An example of a secondary group is a committee organized to plan a holiday party at work. Members of the committee meet infrequently and for only a short period of time. Although group members may have some similar interests, the purpose of the group is about the task instead of the relationships. Sometimes, secondary groups become pretty informal, and the members get to know each other fairly well. Even so, their friendships exist in a limited context; they won't necessarily remain close beyond the holiday party.

Reference Groups

The last type of group we'll discuss in this lesson is a reference group. Reference groups are groups that we look to for guidance in order to evaluate our behaviors and attitudes. They are basically generalized versions of role models. You may or may not belong to the group, but you use its standards of measurement as a frame of reference. For example, if a teenager wants to know if she is slim enough, she may use supermodels as a reference. Or, if a recent college graduate is unsure if an offered salary is fair, he may use the average starting salary of graduates from his school as a reference.

A territory is a term for types of administrative division, usually an area that is under the jurisdiction of a state. In most countries' terminology, such as the United States and Nigeria, it refers to an organized division of an area that is under control of a country but not formally developed into, or incorporated into, a political unit of that country of equal status to other political units such as states or provinces. In international politics, the term is used particularly in reference to a non-sovereign geographic area that has come under the authority of another government; which has not been granted the powers of self-government normally devolved to secondary territorial divisions.

COHESIVENESS

There are different ways to define group cohesion, depending on how researchers conceptualize this concept. However, most researchers define cohesion to be task commitment and interpersonal attraction to the group.

Cohesion can be more specifically defined as the tendency for a group to be in unity while working towards a goal or to satisfy the emotional needs of its members. This definition includes important aspects of cohesiveness, including its multidimensionality dynamic nature, instrumental basis, and emotional dimension. Its multidimensionality refers to how cohesion is based on many factors. Its dynamic nature refers to how it gradually changes over time in its strength and form from the time a group is formed to when a group is disbanded. Its instrumental basis refers to how people cohere for some purpose, whether it be for a task or for social reasons. Its emotional dimension refers to how cohesion is pleasing to its group members. This definition can be generalized to most groups characterized by the group definition discussed above. These groups include sports teams, work groups, military units, fraternity groups, and social groups. However, it is important to note that other researchers claim that cohesion cannot be generalized across many groups.

PRIMARY TERRITORY

Written by Pam MS, NCSP Fact checked by Psychology Dictionary staff As defined in social psychology, the primary territory is a locale controlled and defined by a person or group that uses it for essential existence. While it is similar to the primary environment but holds a subtle difference. Think of a house or dwelling space.

PRIMARY TERRITORY: "Alexander and his wife regarded their house and yard as their primary territory."

SECONDARY TERRITORY

The area is regularly made use of by an individual or group of people who do not have sole possession or control of it. Patrons can exhibit possessive feelings or behavior while still acknowledging the claims of other patrons. Compare with: primary territory; public territory. See also: proxemics. For animal behavior patterns, see: home range

SECONDARY TERRITORY: "The kids considered the mall as their secondary territory."

SOCIABILITY

The quality of being sociable. "For all his sociability, he never really connects with people" Translate sociability to Use over time for sociability

SOCIOGRAM

A sociogram is a graphic representation of social links that a person has. It is a graph drawing that plots the structure of interpersonal relations in a group situation.

COHESIVENESS

THIS CHAPTER WILL DISCUSS:

- How cohesiveness is a result of all the forces that attract people to groups.
- How some of these forces, including liking, identification with the group, and psychological needs, affect maintenance-based cohesiveness.

- How other forces, such as group and personal goals and attraction to group activities, affect task-based cohesiveness.
- How cohesiveness affects diverse group variables, such as group process and productivity.
- What groups can to do increase cohesiveness.

INTRODUCTION

"Cohesiveness" is a term that describes one of the maintenance variables of groups. What does it mean to say that a group is cohesive? Like many concepts, cohesiveness is easy to recognize but difficult to define. People intuitively understand the term. However, it is difficult to define it precisely to everyone's satisfaction.

Cohesive groups have several positive qualities that we all can recognize and agree upon. For example, cohesive groups have a general perception of "we-ness." There is a feeling of friendship and loyalty among group members. The group also has high morale. However, it is problematic to use these qualities to describe the concept of cohesiveness. For example, "morale" is a troublesome term in itself that is difficult to define. Also, a list of qualities will not serve as a definition. How, then, can we define cohesiveness? Scientists have suggested several definitions for the term. In this book, however, we will adopt only one of these suggestions.

The definition of cohesiveness that we will employ comes from the "group dynamics" school of researchers. This school flourished in the 1950s and was a descendant of the work of the great psychologist Kurt Lewin. We have already described some of his work in Chapter 2, and we will continue to refer to him throughout the book. Lewin suggested a definition of cohesiveness that focuses our attention on the individual within the group. He believed that the term depends on how the individual member perceives his or her relationship with a particular group.

Field Theory

Lewin's hypotheses about groups are part of a more general proposal he called "field theory." Field theory examines the relationship between a person's goals and his or her behaviors in pursuit of those goals. For example, Ed wants to graduate from college with honors. How does he work toward that goal and why does he act the way he does in order to reach it?

Lewin proposed a model in order to represent this relationship between goals and behaviors. The model includes all of the factors that affect a person at a given time. These factors are primarily psychological, such as the person's goals and impressions of the current situation. For example, a factor for Ed might be that sometimes it is more fun to play basketball than to study. Ed must deal with the conflicting forces of something that he considers fun at the moment and something that he believes is a good long-term goal. In addition, Lewin's model includes those biological and physical factors that significantly influence a person's psychological state. For instance, Ed might feel so sick one day that he cannot study as much as he thinks he should.

Factors exist at the centers of "regions" within a person's living space. The factors include the person's possible goals, as well as other influences. The areas within the diagram illustrate these regions. The relative locations of the areas represent the relationship that exists between the person (labeled "P" on the model) and the various factors in his or her life (labeled "G"). Regions can have the additional quality of "valences." These are attractive or repulsive characteristics. The characteristics have "forces." In the diagram, the arrows portray the forces at work. They affect the person's movement around his or her life-space.

A region that has a positive valence has the label "+" on the model. It "produces" forces that induce the person toward its center. In contrast, the negatively valenced region creates forces that impede the person's progress toward its center. It has a "-" label on it. For example, the diagram could illustrate a day when Ed found that a basketball game was more attractive to him than the idea of studying for an exam. He might have thought that he already knew the exam material. Whatever the case, the option to study became the "G-" in the model. Ed wanted to avoid doing it. The

"G+" represented the basketball game. As you can clearly see, all the arrows point toward the "G+"; Ed's tendency will be to play basketball that day. (Lewin's model is summarized well by Levinger)

Field Theory and Cohesiveness

A field theorist believes that a "group" has a special place in the life-space model. It exists at the center of its own region in each group member's life-space. For instance, a group called "The Study Group" might consist of Ed, Joan, Mike, and Kim. All four people have unique life-space situations. For each of them, "The Study Group" has a specific place at the center of one of the areas in his or her life-space. The area has a valence that depends on the member's goals and the member's perception concerning whether or not the group can fulfill those goals.

If a group member perceives that the group can fulfill his or her goals, the group becomes attractive. It has a positive valence. There can be various degrees of this attraction. However, to the extent that the group has any positive valence at all, forces in the member's life-space will drive the member toward the group's region. These forces increase the member's attraction toward the group. For example, Ed may want to study mathematics in a group setting.

Further, Ed wants to talk with Kim, because he is attracted to her. He also wants to get to know more students who are serious about their studies. He sees "The Study Group" as something that can fulfill those goals. All of his various goals, combined with his perception that the group can fulfill them in some way, act as forces that increase Ed's attraction to "The Study Group."

The overall cohesiveness of a group is the sum of these positive forces in each member's life-space. Cohesiveness is "the resultant of all forces acting on all the members to remain in the group" (Cartwright, 1968, p. 91). This is the definition that we will be using throughout this book.

For instance, if Joan and Mike have goals that are similar to Ed's, they probably also have strong forces working on them that attract them to "The Study Group." In that case, it would be a very cohesive group. However, it may be that Kim is not very interested in studying in a group because she already knows mathematics very well. She would prefer to study alone. Or perhaps she already has a group of friends that she enjoys very much. She does not want to find a group of similar people, as Ed does. In these cases "The Study Group" will not be so cohesive as it would have been if all members had strong forces working on them to remain in the group.

Distinctions among six perspectives that theorists take toward groups. We called one of these the "motivational" approach. Motivational viewpoint theorists see group behavior as a result of factors that prompt individual behavior, such as needs or goals. Lewin's idea of forces moving people around their life-space is an example of the motivational approach.

Member Commitment

It is important that we do not become confused about the difference between a group's overall amount of cohesiveness and each member's attraction to the group. After all, it makes no sense to talk about individual cohesiveness. To make this distinction clear, we will distinguish between group cohesiveness and member commitment to the group. Moreland and Levine (1982)

have discussed the idea of member commitment to the group in great depth. In their view, a member is committed to the group to the extent that the member is getting what they want from the group more or less than they would get from other groups. If Mike feels that he is getting more from "The Study Group" than from any other comparable group, he will remain a member. If Kim feels she could get more from another group, she will leave.

Moreland and Levine describe how people consider both the present, past, and future when deciding if they want to remain a member of a group. In other words, one weighs whether one is presently getting more from the group than from other groups, if one got more from the group than other groups in the past, and if one expects to get more from the group than from others in the future when making their decision. The theorists feel that in general, present experiences are the most important in determining a person's commitment to a group because what is happening at the present is normally what is most salient in people's minds. Similarly, past experiences are usually more important than future expectations just because they are real experiences the person had.

There are however exceptions to these generalities. When a person has just joined a group, there is no past experience, so the person must decide based on present experiences and expectations about the future.

Analogously, if a person is ready to leave a group, there is no future, so the decision is based on present and past experiences only. Although Moreland and Levine do not consider this, it follows from their analysis that every member makes these same considerations and, as a result, each member has a certain degree of commitment to the group. Thus group cohesiveness depends on how committed each member is to the group as a whole.

COHESIVENESS AS AN OUTPUT VARIABLE

Cohesiveness is a particularly interesting variable to study because it has a dual role in group processes. Clearly, it stands as one of the major output variables in the group process. A group can become cohesive or noncohesive over time. In addition, however, cohesiveness acts as an input variable that affects later group activity. Members of a cohesive group act differently together than members of a noncohesive organization. Hence, cohesiveness has a dual role as both an input and an output variable.

We will first discuss the role of cohesiveness as an output variable. In doing this, we will make a distinction between two different aspects of cohesiveness. The distinction has been made by Tziner (1982) and is consistent with the task versus maintenance distinction that we use throughout this book. One aspect of cohesiveness is based on group members' liking for one another and on their desire to be in the group. We will call

This aspect is "maintenance-based" cohesiveness. For example, several people may form a group because they are attracted to one another. One reason Joan might want to be in "The Study Group" is because she likes the other members. One reason Mike might want to be in "The Study Group" is because he just enjoys the experience of being with other people.

The other aspect of cohesiveness is based on the extent to which the group helps its members reach important goals or participate in desired activities. We will call this aspect "task-based" cohesiveness. Sometimes many members of the group share the same goal. For example, Ed, Joan, and Mike find the idea of studying in a group attractive because they think it will help them understand mathematics better. The group satisfies their desire for this understanding. In addition, a member might join because the group is a means for satisfying "personal goals." In other words, the person attempts to use the group to satisfy goals that other members may not share. For instance, Ed wants to meet Kim because he finds her attractive. That is not a group goal, but Ed thinks that joining the group will still satisfy this desire.

In Chapter 1 we made the claim that cohesiveness is a maintenance variable. Readers should not confuse that claim with what we are saying now. We are saying that there are two aspects of cohesiveness. One aspect is caused by task-based factors and the other aspect is caused by maintenance-based factors.

Maintenance-Based Cohesiveness

As we have noted, a group's cohesiveness is measured by the sum total of the forces attracting its members to it. Many scholars have considered the amount of liking among the members to be the most significant of these forces. If the members do not enjoy being with one another, it probably would be very difficult for them to be attracted to the group. In fact, according to Lott and Lott (1965), one would not lose too much by defining "cohesiveness" simply as the extent to which each group member likes each other member.

Researchers have generally acted as if they agreed with this claim. In a large majority of cases, scientists have actually used "liking" among members as the sole measurement of group cohesiveness. They have similarly used liking as the main method of manipulating cohesiveness. Hence, in practice, most scientists have acted as if cohesiveness and liking are the same in a group. Although we do not agree with this claim, we do recognize the central importance of liking in determining group cohesiveness. For this reason, our discussion regarding liking will be extensive.

Liking

Many researchers have examined the processes that may lead one person to find another person likable. One of these researchers, Newcomb (1960), created a method for classifying the reasons that can lead to one person liking or disliking another person. In his system, there are three general "reasons" that Person A may like or dislike Person B.

Admiration

First, Person A may perceive certain qualities in Person B that Person A likes. Person A may also see things that he or she dislikes. These qualities affect whether A likes B. They are specific "reasons" for liking, and Newcomb grouped them together. He labeled this category the degree of *admiration* that exists between the two people.

Reciprocation.

Second, Person A may like Person B because A believes, in turn, that B likes A. This circular effect can also work to make people dislike each other. Newcomb called this reason reciprocation.

Similarity.

Third, Person A may like or dislike Person B according to how Person A thinks Person B feels about the topic under discussion. If A thinks they agree, A might like B. In contrast, if Person A thinks they disagree,

A may dislike B. It is a question of *similarity* of feelings about X. Before we begin to examine these reasons for liking, we must briefly explain the idea of contact. As we all know, Person A cannot come to like Person B unless they meet each other in the first place.

Contact

People come to like only those people they have

the opportunity to meet. This claim is intuitively obvious. Even so, we should not ignore its importance. There have been many studies examining the importance of contact as it relates to liking, and they have had some interesting results.

One thing we know is that the odds that people will come into contact with each other is a function of the extent to which they are located near each other. This physical nearness is significant. Many studies have shown that friendships at school or work are more likely to form among people who sit near each other, as opposed to those who sit far away from each other. This is also true among people who live near one another. These findings are clearly relevant to liking in small groups. People in groups are unquestionably in contact with one another. Therefore the potential is there for group members to come to like one another, increasing the odds of a cohesive group.

Initial meetings and likability.

However, contact with other members in a decision-making group is often involuntary. It might seem that increased contact when it is involuntary, would also increase the odds that people will come to *dis*like one another. One could hypothesize that group members would resent being forced together. However, scientists have found that dislike is relatively rare among new acquaintances. Indeed, it appears that people expect to like other people they meet. There seems to be a bias within people toward mutually liking one another until they see a good reason not to do so. One could say that people find one another "likable" until proven otherwise.

A study by Darley and Berscheid (1967) examined this idea. Their study led some women to anticipate that they would take part in a dyadic discussion. The topic would be dating behavior. The researchers then showed the women information about their "fictional" partners. They also showed them data concerning an additional fictional participant in the experiment. These two sets of information were identical. The study then asked the women to evaluate the fictional participants. The women expressed more liking for, as well as a greater desire to work with, their future "partner" than for the other fictional "woman," despite the fact that the data about the two fictional women had been identical. It appears that the anticipation of meeting a person leads to the expectation of liking that person. This works at least until

further information about the person comes to light. The study implies that, when someone assigns us to a group, we generally come to the first meeting expecting to like the other members.

Admiration

As we said earlier, one reason why Person A may like Person B is that Person A perceives certain qualities in Person B that Person A likes. Analogously, Person A may dislike Person B because A sees qualities in B that A dislikes. We call the perceptions we have about another person's qualities our *personality impression* of that other person.

Personality impressions are probably the biggest factor in long-term liking. These impressions are the mental pictures we have of people. These mental pictures consist of descriptions of what kind of people they are, what they look like, what kinds of things they do, and so on. Apparently, our beliefs about people's permanent characteristics--the kind of people they are--have a great impact on whether we like them.

The beliefs that we hold about a person exist as a network of *traits*. These traits are mostly adjectives that are meant to describe a person's personality and character. There are many trait terms that we use to describe personality. For example, we might call a person "nice," "clumsy," "attractive," or "weak." It is important to realize that traits are abstractions. They are generalized terms for a set of behaviors, but they are not behaviors themselves. For example, you cannot see a "clumsy." What you can see is an action that you can classify as "clumsy." The classification is a decision of sorts. It is not inherent in the behavior (Reeder & Brewer, 1979). After all, conduct that is "clumsy" in most instances may be "smart" in some circumstances. For example, dropping a glass may seem to be a clumsy behavior, but it is a smart action if the glass is hot enough to burn you badly.

We use the behaviors that we see people perform in order to form our impressions of them. At a party, a person might perform a series of behaviors that we consider clumsy. For example, the person drops a glass, spills popcorn, and dances on his or her partner's feet.

After noticing this behavior, we then judge whether performing behaviors of that type is an inherent part of the person's personality. We could instead decide that the behavior is a momentary lapse caused by circumstance. For example, when we see the person dropping the glass and spilling the popcorn, we might think that the person is naturally clumsy. In contrast, we might believe that the person could be drunk or nervous. In other words, we must decide whether the person's Character or the circumstance is responsible for the clumsiness.

Theorists have put a lot of thought into determining the conditions under which observers see a person's character as responsible for his or her actions. Jones and Davis (1965) examined what happened when observers saw the behavior only once. In this case, onlookers assign responsibility for the action to the extent that the behavior is unexpected, unusual, or unexplainable by circumstance. For example, one-day people see Ted complaining about standing in a line at the bookstore. If Ted is late for an appointment or if the line seems unusually long to everybody in it, observers may say that the circumstance is responsible for Ted being impatient. If the line is short and to be expected, Ted's complaints are unusual. In that case, onlookers might say that Ted has the personality trait of being an impatient person.

Kelley (1967) described examples of behavior that occurred in different situations. Observers had more than one example that they could use to form a judgment. In such a circumstance, observers assign responsibility for the behavior to the extent that the action is similar across situations, consistent with different people, and different from the norm. For example, onlookers see Ted in many situations, and he is consistently complaining about having to wait. He complains too many people and in inappropriate situations. Other people complain far less about waiting than Ted. This series of behaviors may lead the observers to consider Ted's character to be that of an impatient person.

Once we judge that the person's character is responsible for the behavior, we attribute the relevant trait to the person. For example, we attribute the trait of impatience to Ted. Thus, we call the work of Jones, Kelley, and their associate's attribution theory.

Let us return to the example of the clumsy person at the party. If the circumstances apply, we could decide that the person has the character trait of clumsiness. Having made this attribution, we tentatively assign other traits to this person to the extent that clumsiness implies the new traits. For example, we could believe that clumsiness is associated with stupidity. In that case, we would also expect to see "stupid" actions from this person.

Researchers call this tendency the "halo effect" when it applies to "good" attributes and the "horns effect" when it involves "bad" character traits. For example, in one study, researchers showed participants photographs and then asked them to make judgments about the person photographed. The participants saw more attractive people as being more intelligent and more exciting to be with than less attractive people. The "good" characteristic "attractive" led to the assignment of other "good"

Characteristics of the person. The halo effect is not all-powerful, however. If you later recognize "smart" behavior, for example, from the person you judged "clumsy," you can change your impression of the person. However, the person you thought clumsy must behave clearly in a way that is "smart," for it is difficult to alter initial impressions.

We gradually build up a unique impression of a person as time passes. This impression comes from our own observations of the person and from our interpretations of what we hear about him or her from other people (Hewes et al., 1985). As we have shown, various factors and situations come into play as this "impression formation" process takes place.

First, we feel a need to be able to explain and predict other people's behavior. Traits help us explain and predict. They can give us an intuitively satisfying explanation for behaviors. For instance, Jacob dropped a glass because he is "clumsy." We do not need to worry about a further explanation. In addition, traits are a device we can use to predict later behavior. Because Jacob is clumsy, we better not invite him into a china shop.

Second, we use traits because they serve as a basis for evaluating a person. This is crucial to our interest in liking and admiration. For example, we may think badly of clumsiness. We believe that Jacob is clumsy. It follows that we have a reason to think badly of Jacob. Of course, we assign quite a few attributes to a person. The way that we evaluate one trait may contradict our evaluation of another trait. For example, we might also think that Jacob is "funny." We evaluate that trait as being a good attribute. Because we like "funny" people, we may think well of Jacob because he is funny.

Researchers have tried to predict our overall "liking" of a person who has several traits that we evaluate differently. Quite a lot of work has gone into developing algebraic formulas to answer those questions. The best-known model holds that whether we like a person depends on the average of the evaluations of the individual traits. Each evaluation is weighted according to the importance of the trait (Anderson, 1974). This model serves fairly well, but a few cases elude it. Sometimes combinations of traits lead to unique situations that do not occur when each attribute occurs separately.

For example, if someone tells you that Jill is "dumb" and "blonde," the two traits together may create a rather negative picture in your mind. Without meeting Jill,

You may think her to be "flighty" or "irresponsible." However, if the person only says that Jill is "blonde," you might think Jill to be "friendly" and "exciting" because she is blonde. Similarly, the combination of "dishonest" and "generous" is another instance in which a unique combination changes things. These traits may lead to a picture of a Robin Hood-type character with a particularly positive overall evaluation.

Impressions and evaluations of the personalities of people are very important in a small group. They influence the manner in which group members interact. Certain impressions have considerable significance in the small group setting. One type is the attribution of intelligence and competence. Suls and Miller (1978) conducted a study concerning this. They had their participants take an exam that tested their "ability" at social psychology. They then rated them as either "very good," "good," "average," or "poor" at social psychology skills. The researchers asked the participants to choose the type of person with whom they would wish to form study groups. Not surprisingly, 93.1 and 89.4 percent of the participants in two respective studies wanted partners who were rated either "very good" or "good."

Reciprocation

As we have discussed, one of the most important factors in the degree to which Cisco, for example, likes Kristin, is the degree to which Kristin likes Cisco.

Researchers call this process "reciprocation." There are many possible reasons that Cisco will tend to reciprocate Kristin's liking. The approval that Cisco gets from Kristin, as a sole factor, should cause Cisco to return Kristin's liking. In addition, Cisco can look forward to cooperation and support from Kristin. This adds to Cisco's reciprocation.

We can see how this could work in a small group. For example, the group leader may give compliments or criticisms to a group member. These might give the member an impression of the extent to which the leader likes or dislikes the member. The impression will, in turn, influence the member to reciprocate in a similar way. Indeed, many studies have used criticisms and compliments in order to support the tendency for the degree of liking to be reciprocated.

In fact, one study showed compliments and criticisms to be directly related to group cohesiveness. Dittes (1959) asked groups of participants to discuss a problem concerning juvenile delinquency and interrupted the discussion on three occasions to allow members to rate how desirable they found one another as group members. After the discussion, each participant was shown what was said to be the other members' ratings of her or him. Actually, the participants were shown phony ratings that implied they were either accepted or rejected by the other members. After a second group discussion,

the members were asked how much they wanted to remain in the group. Participants who thought they had been accepted were more attracted to the group than participants who thought they had been rejected.

In congruency.

The incongruency exception occurs when Person A believes that Person B's praise or blame is inconsistent with Person A's own self-appraisal. For example, Cisco may think poorly of himself. However, he believes that Kristin likes him. In such a situation, Cisco may believe that Kristin's judgment is faulty because he believes that she is wrong to like him. He will then dislike her as well as her opinion. Deutsch and Solomon (1959) performed an experiment that highlighted the incongruency problem. They had their participants perform as "members" of two "teams." They then gave their participants phony evaluations of their performances, rating them either good or bad. Each participant next wrote a note to one of his or her "teammates." The researchers collected the real notes but gave fake notes back to the participants. These phony notes indicated that the "teammate" either did or did not want the participant on their "team" in the future. The participants next made written evaluations of the "teammates" who they thought had written notes to them.

Results of the study showed that participants thought a great deal about their own performance rating as they read their fake notes. Each participant kept in Mind his or her "grade" in the experiment. Participants who believed that they had performed well-liked their "teammate" the most if the note writer wanted the participant to stay on the "team." In contrast, these "good" performers liked the "teammate" least if he or she wanted the participant of the "team."

This process did not take place if the participants believed that they had not done well. These "bad" performers reported that their liking for the "teammate" was intermediate. It was unaffected by the "teammate's" evaluation of them. Neither liking nor disliking was reciprocated. It appears that when somebody knows that he or she has performed a task badly, the process of reciprocation is unaffected. The tendency to return verbal approval may be offset by the knowledge that the approver is wrong.

However, the interpretation of this study does lead to some problems. Berscheid and Walster (1978) point out some of them. If Person B praises Person A after a bad performance, Person A may come to think that Person B is either stupid or insincere. These feelings will affect the reciprocation process in a different way from the congruency exception. The possibility that Person B is insincere leads us to the second exception regarding reciprocation.

Ingratiation.

The ingratiation exception occurs when Person A comes to believe that Person B's praise is due to some ulterior motive for gaining Person A's favor. For example, Cisco believes that Kristin is praising him in order to get later rewards from him. The ingratiation exception is most likely to occur if Cisco has reason to believe that Kristin's words are false. This is most likely to happen when Cisco is confident about the degree to which he possesses the characteristic on which Kristin's praise is based.

For example, it is useless to compliment people on their looks if they know that they are good-looking. They have heard it before and probably do not want to hear it again. It is equally useless to compliment people on their looks if they know for certain that they are not good-looking. They will know that the compliment is a lie.

There are perhaps times when a person can succeed in using false praise to be ingratiating. The most successful time would be when the person being praised does not know their qualities well. For example, perhaps a person does not know whether he or she is really good-looking (Jones, 1964). In such a case, ingratiation may create liking. The person does not perceive that the compliment is false. He or she does not suspect any ulterior motive and liking can occur through reciprocation.

Similarity

Newcomb included "similarity" within his typology system. He believed it was a cause for liking. The idea refers to the pleasure that one feels when interacting with someone who has similar beliefs and opinions as oneself. The attitudinal agreement, along with reciprocity of liking, is particularly important in the establishment of casual friendships. As such, it is extremely important in the small-group setting. Small groups often involve casual relationships.

Newcomb (1960, 1961) explored this issue in a classic study of the acquaintance process. For the study, Newcomb obtained the use of a boarding house near the University of Michigan campus. On two occasions he invited 17 male transfer students to live there for a semester free of charge. In exchange, Newcomb required them to participate in four to five hours of research a week. He performed various studies with the groups. Some of the experiments explored the patterns of the friendships that formed and the reasons for the friendships.

Early in the semester, functional distance and reciprocation of liking were the major determinants of liking. This was expected. Students were attracted to students who were close to them and who seemed to like them in return. However, attitude similarity became a critical factor as the semester progressed. As the students.got to know one another better, they learned how they all really felt. Opinions came out into the open. As this happened, the students started to like others who shared their attitudes. They also lessened in their liking for those who did not agree with them about topics.

The relationship between the extent to which people believe they agree with one another and the extent to which they like one another is extremely strong. Byrne (1971) and his coworkers conducted a series of studies that showed how strong that relationship can be. Byrne's research centered on a basic experimental procedure. For his studies, participants rated their attitudes toward each of 26 political, social, and religious issues. Several weeks later, the experimenters gave the participants a set of ratings for these same issues. They told them that the ratings were those of a stranger they were to meet. The researchers then asked

The participants to rate their liking for the unknown person and their willingness to work with him or her on a project. The participants also rated the stranger on other characteristics, such as intelligence and character. What the participants did not know was that there was no actual "stranger." Instead, the researchers had given them a list based upon the participants' own opinions. The experimenters wrote down opinions that agreed or disagreed with the attitudes of the participants in a predetermined way. The lists ranged from total agreement, through proportions of agreement, to total disagreement. The study found that the degree of liking of the unknown person was strongly related to the proportion of statements on which the participant and the "stranger" agreed. In addition, greater accord led to a halo effect. Participants also rated an "agreeing" stranger as more intelligent, well-informed, moral, and well adjusted than a "disagreeing" person.

In his later studies, Byrne found this relationship to hold for people of all ages and socioeconomic groups. It also was true for people from different countries and even for hospitalized schizophrenics. In all the cases, the perceived agreement led to a liking of the "stranger." However, as with any such relationship, there are exceptions.

One exception is that, if the topic of agreement or disagreement is not important, it has no effect on liking. This is particularly true if the people interacting talk about other topics that they consider important. For example, Cisco and Kristin might disagree about their favorite colors, but they agree about the person they should elect a president. The topic of their favorite colors is not important, and it does not figure into whether they like each other. The topic of the presidential candidate is important to them, however, and because they agree about that, they probably will like each other.

Another exception that Byrne found was that agreement with a person with undesirable qualities has no effect on liking. For example, you may agree with a drug addict who says that nuclear disarmament is good. However, if you do not like the lifestyle of a person dependent on drugs, you will probably not become friends with the drug addict even though you agree with his or her opinion.

The similarity in opinions has been directly related to group cohesiveness. Festinger (1954) reported a study he performed with Gerard, Hymovitch, Kelley, and Raven in which groups studied a labor dispute and then evaluated the union's decisions in the dispute. Afterward, each member was asked how much they thought other group members agreed with them about the dispute and how much they attracted they were to the group. Those members who thought they agreed with the other members were more attracted to the group than hose members who thought they disagreed.

Conclusions.

Liking is the most important element in maintenance-based group cohesiveness. It is a powerful force that influences whether people want to be with one another. As such, it has an impact on whether a group is drawn together cohesively. Research into the topic of liking has revealed a variety of factors that affect the processes of how and why one person finds another person likable. All of these factors come into play in a group setting. There are other forces, however, that affect maintenance-based cohesiveness.

Identification with the Group

Sometimes, our membership in a group becomes a very important part of our self-identity. For example, Karintha is a member of a basketball team called the {Sharks}. When she thinks about herself, one of the first things that come to Karintha's mind is "I am a Shark." In this situation, we can say that Karintha *identifies* with the Sharks. According to Hogg (1992), when we identify with a group we look favorably upon the other members of the group, even those we do not find particularly likable. This is particularly true when circumstances make us think about our group membership. Nadine is also a member of the Sharks. Karintha does not find Nadine especially likable. However, if Karintha hears an outsider criticizing Nadine's performance as a Shark, Karintha is likely to jump to Nadine's defense. According to Hogg, although Karintha does not like Nadine, Karintha identifies with Nadine because they are members of the same team. Hogg called Karintha's feelings toward Nadine *social attraction* to distinguish it from regular liking.

Hogg and associates (Hogg & Hardie, 1991; Hogg, Cooper-Shaw, & Holzworth Hogg felt that liking and social attraction have separate effects on group cohesiveness. It is possible that each is a more important factor than the other in determining group cohesiveness in different circumstances. It would follow from Hogg's claims that when group members identify strongly with their group, cohesiveness would depend more on how much social attraction group members have for one another than on how much they like one another. In contrast, when group members do not identify with their group very much, cohesiveness would depend more on mutual liking. Research to evaluate these ideas needs to be performed before we can have confidence in them.

Psychological Needs

There has always been speculation that people may be attracted to a group in order to satisfy some deep- seated psychological need. As we discussed in Chapter 1, McClelland (1961) hypothesized that some people have a particular high need for affiliation with others. It follows that people high on this need would be likely to want to be a member of a group. Thus the extent to which group members have a need for affiliation would be a factor in the amount of maintenance-based cohesiveness in their group. Similarly, McClelland also believed that some people have a particular high need for power. One can imagine that a person who has a strong desire to dominate others may join a group in order to take a leadership role. Being leader would satisfy his or her need to be in charge. The group will continue to be attractive only as long as the person can successfully dominate the other members.

A group member's desire to satisfy such psychological needs may indirectly affect cohesiveness through its direct effect on group process. Imagine that a group contains a member who has a very strong desire to dominate. Picture what his or her communication would be like. As you can envision, this communication would probably have a great effect on the other members' attraction to the group. What exactly would this communication be like? Would the group member who desires to be in charge try to make the other group members feel worthless? Or would he or she feel secure as leader and try to make the group attractive to the other members.

Communication and status needs.

A study by Kelley (1951) suggests some answers to these questions. He theorized that people desire to have high status in their groups. His idea was that most people have the psychological need to have status. Kelley further hypothesized that this desire affects the type of communication that group members exchange. He divided eight-member groups into two four-member subgroups. The researcher then told the subgroups that one of them would receive a series of patterns of rectangles. He gave them instructions that they were to write messages to the second subgroup that would help the second subgroup reproduce the patterns. The researcher also said that group members could write notes to one another within their subgroups. The messages did not have to be limited to technical information. The members of each subgroup then went into different rooms. The researcher said he would give them their assignments and take their messages back and forth for them.

The participants thought the experiment would be as the researcher had described it to them. In actuality, he never delivered the real messages. Instead, the experimenter collected all the participants' notes and gave out phony ones he had written himself. Further, he assigned both groups the task of reproducing patterns. There was no "sending" subgroup. Most important, Kelley told participants about the status and the permanence of their jobs. He assigned each participant a job, as a message translator or a pattern reproducer. He told them that the former was a high-status job and that the latter was a low-status task.

Kelley then analyzed the messages that the participants sent one another. The notes sent to the fictional "sending" subgroup revealed differences among the group members. The researcher determined that the high-status/nonmobile and the low status/mobile participants sent more "cohesiveness-building" messages than other members. Their notes contained overtures to friendship, encouragement, and praise and other such statements. Kelley interpreted these results under the assumption that the participants wanted to have high status if they felt they could attain it. The high-status/nonmobile participants knew that they would retain their status, and so were comfortable sending cohesiveness-building messages to the other subgroup. The low-status/mobile participants probably thought that sending these messages might help them gain high status. In contrast, Kelley believed that the high-status/mobile participants probably felt their status threatened and so refrained from encouraging the other members. Finally, the low-status/nonmobile participants were resigned to their fate and saw no point in sending cohesiveness- building messages. These latter two group members sent far fewer messages that were designed to build cohesiveness.

Interestingly, within the subgroups these patterns changed. In their own groups, the mobile members sent more "cohesiveness-building" messages than the nonmobile members did. This was true no matter what their status was.Unfortunately, it is impossible to determine the effect of the members' notes on one another. Because no member ever received the actual notes, the study could not examine whether the notes affected the receiver's attraction to the subgroup. However, the study did reveal that group members communicated differently, based on their status and ability to change that status. These different types of communication could affect group cohesiveness.

Evaluation needs.

There is also some evidence that people want to be with others in order to learn more about themselves. Festinger's (1954) theory of social comparison proposes that people have a desire to evaluate their own abilities. We will be explaining this theory more fully in Chapter 6, "Conformity and Deviance," but Festinger's idea has applications for this section also.

Singer and Shockley (1965) conducted an experiment to test Festinger's idea. They asked 38 participants to complete a phony task. The participants then received a number representing their "score" on the task. The researchers gave 24 of them an interpretation of the meaning of the score. Out of these 24, only 2 chose to wait with other participants while the researchers set up a second part of the experiment. In contrast, 6 of the 14 who had not received an interpretation of their scores wanted to wait with other participants. They could then talk among themselves. It appeared that the people who did not know how well they had done felt the desire to associate with others who had done the task.

As we have discussed, group membership in itself may be attractive to some humans because membership can satisfy various psychological needs. In particular, needs for affiliation, power and status, and knowledge about themselves may draw people into groups. Therefore, needs such as these can be a factor in maintenance-based cohesiveness.

Task-Based Cohesiveness

As we mentioned earlier, task-based cohesiveness can be the result of group members' desires to achieve either group or personal goals or the members' attraction to group activities. Studies have been performed in order to understand the impact of these factors.

Group Goals

A group might attract a person if the group has an attractive goal. A classic study reported in Sherif and Sherif (1953) showed this tendency at work. The study took place at a summer camp for 12-year-old boys. Experimenters first established intergroup hostility between the boys. The researchers then strove to evaluate various methods for reducing this hostility.

The study divided the boys into two groups, called the "Bull Dogs" and the "Red Devils." Each group lived in a different part of the camp and performed its necessary activities, such as food preparation, separately. To create Intergroup hostility, the researchers arranged games, contests, and circumstances in such a way that one group interfered with the activities of the other. These methods succeeded in arousing a great deal of animosity. Name- calling and fights broke out.

COHESIVENESS AS AN INPUT VARIABLE

Thus far we have conceived of cohesiveness as a result of several factors. As such it is an output variable. There is good reason for this. When a group first begins, there is little or no cohesiveness. However, once a group has been together for some time, some level of cohesiveness is established. This level of cohesiveness will then become a factor in subsequent group discussion. Hence, it will become an input variable. As such a variable, it will be mediated through group discussion. When this takes place, it can affect all of the output variables we have discussed in this book. Cohesiveness can even indirectly affect itself.Cohesiveness, Communication, and Social Influence

Lott and Lott's Study

It stands to reason that members of groups that are cohesive are likely to talk with one another more than members of noncohesive groups. It also stands to reason that group cohesiveness would affect the process of "social influence." We will describe "social influence" further in Chapter 7. For now, we can simply say that "social influence" refers to the ways in which group members influence one another's beliefs, attitudes, and behaviors. Cohesiveness should affect attempts at social influence during group discussions, and these attempts should alter group members' attitudes after the discussion is over.

Lott and Lott (1961) presented evidence that seems consistent with these claims. They asked 15 ongoing campus groups of 6 to 10 members to discuss whether or not students are too contented, lazy, and self- centered. They measured how much communication occurred. They also asked group members' opinions about this issue both before and after the discussion, to see if the discussion led to the members changing these opinions. Finally, they asked group members how much they liked one another in order to measure group cohesiveness. They found that high liking among the members led to greater amounts of talk about the issue under consideration. In turn, there was a significant group influence on member opinions concerning the issue. Members' opinions became closer to one another after the discussion in high liking groups.

Unfortunately, Lott and Lott's study underestimates the complexity of the relationship between cohesiveness, communication, and social influence. As mentioned earlier in this chapter, Lott and Lott in another article claimed that liking among members is a sufficient measure of group cohesiveness. Unfortunately, this claim overlooks the distinction between maintenance- and task-based cohesiveness.

Back's Study

A classic study by Back (1951) illustrates the importance of this distinction. Back wanted to see if various factors that cause cohesiveness would affect social influence differently. He used three different manipulations to induce cohesiveness in his dyads, or two-member groups. In the "liking" manipulation, he told the participants that they would either definitely get along with their dyad partner, that they would probably get along, or that they might irritate one another. This first manipulation was clearly an attempt to encourage high versus low versus no maintenance-based cohesiveness. In the "task" manipulation, he either told the participants that the best individual task performer would receive five dollars for their performance or just encouraged them to do the task well. This second manipulation was clearly an attempt to encourage high versus low task-based maintenance. In the "prestige" manipulation, he told the participants that, based on their class work, they should be the best group of all or just a good performing group. It is not clear whether this is a task or maintenance-based manipulation.

In the actual study, Back gave his participants a series of three photographs. He then told them to write a preliminary draft of a story explaining and connecting the photographs. After completing the story, the subjects returned the photographs and then met in groups of two, or dyads. The researcher told the participants that they had written stories about the same pictures and that they were to exchange information so that each could do a better job on subsequent, final stories explaining the photographs. In actuality, each member of a dyad had seen slightly different pictures. This meant that some disagreement between the dyad members was likely. Back analyzed each dyad's interaction to see how much the members communicated and how they attempted to influence each other. He then compared each participant's preliminary and final stories to see whether the partners had actually influenced each other. The findings depended on the type of cohesiveness manipulation. Let us look at these results for different variables in turn.

Amount of communication.

Not surprisingly, the more maintenance-based cohesion in the group, the more the group members talked to one another. Even the dyads told that they would "probably" as one another talked for a relatively long amount of time. This is consistent with the findings of Lott and Lott's (1961) study. However, *low* task-maintenance dyads talked more than high. These participants seemed to view each other merely as tools for achieving good task performance, and the high task-maintenance dyads seemed to feel they did not need to talk much to perform the task well. The hi and low "prestige" groups seemed to act like the "liking" groups in this regard, although they talked a lot less as a whole.

SOCIAL INFLUENCE.

Overall, highly cohesive dyads of all three types engaged in more attempted influence than low-cohesive dyads. The attempts at influence involved stating their own positions, arguing, and reasoning with each other. Similarly, the high-cohesive dyads had more verbal reactions to these influence attempts than did the other dyads. The cohesive partners would agree or disagree with each other, counter argue, and reject each other's stories. Both attempted influence and verbal reactions to these attempts were highest for the "task" manipulation groups, providing more evidence that members of these dyads used each other as tools for achieving good task performance. Finally, there was the more actual influence of One's stories in the high cohesive dyads than the low for the "liking" and "task" manipulations, although cohesiveness had no effect on actual influence in the "prestige" dyads.

IMPLICATIONS.

Back's study leads to some interesting further implications involving the effect of cohesiveness on interaction. It would seem to be intuitively reasonable to predict that the more cohesive a group is, the more "friendly" its conversation will be. One could also expect that such a group will have greater cohesiveness in the future. These predictions do contain some truth. However, Back's results clearly show that they are too simplistic. First, this expected finding did not occur in the "task" groups. Second, the high cohesive groups were more argumentative than the less cohesive groups. Their discussions seemed to arouse a great deal of conflict.

In fact, because of their feeling of being "glued together," a cohesive group should be more likely to engage in any type of unpleasant communication. A study by Pepitone and Reichling (1955) is relevant to this point. Members of dyads were either told they would or would not like one another. Then, a person introduced as "the experimenter" insulted both participants. While subsequently performing a task, the dyads composed of members who had been told they would like one another spent more time expressing hostility about the experimenter and their task to one another than the dyads composed of member who had been told they would not like one another. What we should expect is for communication among members of cohesive groups to be alternatively more friendly and more argumentative and unfriendly than that in noncohesive groups. In fact, in Chapter 8,

"Group Process," we will be describing work by Robert F. Bales that provides an explanation for why this should occur.

Cohesiveness and Satisfaction

Exline (1957) performed an interesting study regarding the role of cohesiveness as an input variable. His experiment is problematic, but it does shed more light on the question of how cohesiveness affects a group. Exline manipulated maintenance-based cohesiveness by telling his participants that, based phony personality measures the subjects had filled out earlier, they would be "congenial" or not be congenial. Exline next had his participants take part in a "role-play" exercise. This was an improvised dramatic situation in which each participant had a secret role to play. In comparison with the less congenial groups, the more congenial groups had members who stated that they had more liking for one another. They also had a greater desire to work together. In addition, they were more satisfied with their performance and better able to guess one another's assigned role in the exercise. The findings appeared to reveal that cohesiveness has a positive effect upon group member satisfaction.

There are problems with this study, however. Exline did not analyze the group's exercises. Therefore, we cannot get a clear picture of the connection that may have existed between the input of cohesiveness and the output of satisfaction. On the one hand, it could be that the more congenial groups actually did do a better job of performing the exercise than the less "congenial" groups. On the other hand, it may be that the more congenial groups did not actually perform better. Perhaps they were more satisfied only because of their cohesiveness. Exline's results do suggest that there is a connection between cohesiveness and satisfaction. However, his study is an example of the ambiguities that result when researchers ignore group process. We need to know more before we can make definite statements.

Cohesiveness and Task Productivity

Our next concern regarding cohesiveness as an input variable involves the relationship between it and task productivity. For many years, this relationship was Considered to be complex and somewhat unclear. Dozens of studies have been performed since the early 1950s, with contradictory findings. Sometimes cohesive groups were more productive than noncohesive groups, sometimes they were less productive, and sometimes cohesiveness did not seem to affect productivity at all.

Recently, it has become evident that considering the distinction between task- and maintenance-based cohesiveness clarifies much of this confusion. A study by Zaccaro and Lowe (1988) reflects this new understanding. The researchers formed four-person groups to perform a productivity task. Before the task, the experimenters carried out manipulations to induce either high or low maintenance-based and task-based cohesiveness. First, half the groups participated in an exercise designed to generate maintenance-based cohesiveness. The group broke up temporarily into dyads who talked to one another, and then all four group members took turns introducing their dyadic partner to the two other members.

The other half of the groups did not perform this exercise, leading to lower maintenance-based cohesiveness. Second, half of the high and half of the low maintenance-based cohesive groups were told about the importance of good performance on their upcoming task and offered extra credit if they were the best performing group. This manipulation was designed to enhance task-

based cohesiveness. The other groups were not told anything, resulting in lower task-based maintenance. As a consequence of these manipulations, the groups were either high or low on task-based cohesiveness and either high or low on maintenance-based cohesiveness. Finally, the group performed the productivity task, which involved folding as many sheets of paper into tent-shaped forms as they could in fifteen minutes. During the performance, the researchers measured how much communication occurred. The researchers also asked the participants how committed they were to performing their task well.

The results showed that groups high on task-based cohesiveness were more committed to task performance and more productive than groups low on task-based cohesiveness. In contrast, groups high and low on maintenance-based cohesiveness were equal in productivity. Interestingly, the groups that were high in maintenance-based cohesiveness were also highly committed to the task. However, consistently with the Lott and Lott (1961) and Back (1951), they were also extremely talkative, and the more talkative groups were less productive. This is just one of several studies that have found that talking hurts performance in productivity tasks. Thus the higher talking canceled out the effects of high motivation in the high maintenance-based cohesive groups.

A review of literature by Mullen & Copper (1994) shows that, in general, cohesive groups are more productive than noncohesive groups, particularly when group size is relatively small. However, this relationship is much stronger for task-based cohesiveness than it is for maintenance-based cohesiveness. Clearly, when groups are cohesive because their members care about their task, they will usually be more productive than groups that are not cohesive because their members do not care about their task.

They performed a study similar to the study by Kelley that we described earlier. However, in Schachter et al.'s experiment, the role of cohesiveness changed from an output to an input variable. In the study, the researchers asked three-women groups to work on producing cardboard checkerboards. The study divided the task into three parts. The task involved cutting the cardboard, pasting it on heavier stock, and painting the checkerboard pattern on it through a stencil. The experimenters said they would assign each participant in the group one of these tasks. The experimenters said that the participants would work in separate rooms, and they could exchange notes via messengers. Researchers also told the participants either that they definitely would or that they might not like their "coworkers." This was a successful manipulation of cohesiveness, based on later ratings for liking. In actuality, the participants all did the same job. Each ended up cutting cardboard.

The experimenters also intercepted their notes and replaced them with a standardized series of messages that they gave the participants every four minutes.

The implication of these findings is that groups high on maintenance-based cohesiveness are susceptible to influence from their group. If their group cares about task performance, they will be productive, and if their group does not care about the task, they will not be productive. In contrast, groups low on maintenance-based cohesiveness are less susceptible to influence from their group, so whether the group cares about task performance will have little effect.

Cohesiveness, Decision Accuracy, and Quality

The relationship of cohesiveness with decision accuracy and quality is not entirely clear. After reviewing past research, Mullen, Anthony, Salas, and Driskell (1994) concluded that task-based cohesiveness led to better decisions, whereas maintenance-based cohesiveness to worse decisions. If true, this finding would be similar to that for cohesiveness and productivity. As in that case, a group that is cohesive because its members care about the task would work harder and thus make better decisions than a group whose members do not care about the task. In contrast, groups that is cohesive because their members like one another may place more emphasis on getting along well with one another than in making a good decision, and as a result make worse decisions than groups whose members do not like one another. In fact, there is reason to believe that, under some conditions, getting along well becomes so important to highly cohesive groups that their members become hesitant to freely exchange ideas. In this circumstance, groups can make disastrously bad decisions. This condition is known as *groupthink*, "Decision Theory."

The problem with this general conclusion is that Mullen et al. did not distinguish between accuracy and quality tasks in their review. It is not clear that their conclusion is true for both types of tasks. For example, Zaccaro and McCoy (1988) performed a study in which they manipulated task- and maintenance-based cohesiveness the same way as in the Zaccaro and Lowe (1988) discussed earlier. Afterward, the groups performed a survival game accuracy task such as the ones we discussed in Chapter 2. Accuracy was highest for groups high in both maintenance- and task-based cohesiveness than in groups low in either or both types of cohesiveness. This finding suggests that accurate tasks may be performed better by groups whose members like one another and care about their tasks. If so, then Mullen et al.'s generalizations are false.

Toward A General Theory of Cohesiveness as Input

We are in far better shape to propose a general theory of cohesiveness as an input variable than we were for cohesiveness as an output variable, because we know more about the role of communication as process in this case. When cohesiveness is due to task factors, members of highly cohesive groups are more dedicated to their task than members of less cohesive groups. Communication is largely task-oriented and, as a consequence, task performance is better for highly cohesive groups. In contrast, when cohesiveness is due to maintenance factors, members of highly cohesive groups may or may not be dedicated to their task. If they are dedicated to their task, they will act like high task-cohesive groups and perform well. If they are not dedicated to their task, their communication will be largely maintenance-oriented, and they will perform more poorly on their task than noncohesive groups.

We see that, as an input variable, cohesiveness has an effect on the social influence process and on task performance. As such, it can be a powerful tool. Increased cohesiveness can lead to more successful groups. Can we influence whether a group is cohesive? In the next section we provide some recommendations.

PUTTING THEORY INTO PRACTICE

There are definite advantages for a group to have members that are attracted to it. Cohesiveness can improve the functioning of the group. Members of highly cohesive groups tend to trust and have confidence in one another. This leads to an atmosphere that allows the expression of conflicting points of view. Such free expression is necessary for the group to make its best possible decision.

Cohesiveness also provides the potential for a group to work at its fastest and most productive levels. Finally, cohesive groups have members who enjoy being together. Interaction in a friendly group creates good feelings. The entire cohesive group experience brings satisfaction. These are valuable goals in and of themselves. We should not forget them even in the face of pressing task requirements.

There is however a bad side to cohesiveness. Cohesiveness that is solely a result of group members liking one another can lead to poor group performance. If the group is more concerned with maintaining good relationships or having a good time with one another, task work will suffer. Therefore, no matter what factors have led to cohesiveness, the group must be motivated to perform its task. If it is, the group should work well together.

As you can see, the cohesive group has a great many good qualities. Unfortunately, one cannot force a group to be cohesive. For example, members may honestly dislike one another, or its members not care about its task. There is little that can be done about this.

However, in most cases, a group can perform specific actions in order to increase its own cohesiveness. The following recommendations may be helpful:

1.The group can increase the amount of communication among its members. The success of this strategy, however, depends on the content of the communication. The strategy will backfire if the extra talk consists mostly of disagreement or expressions of dislike. However, keep in mind that once a group achieves cohesiveness, there is a danger of too much concentration on agreement and good feeling among members. The group must attain a proper balance.

2.The group can elevate the attractiveness of group interaction. For example, encourage some humor during group decision making. This will help counteract the anxieties and pressures brought on by attention to the task. A little fun at the beginning, and particularly at the end, of a meeting is good. In addition, have members perform the less interesting tasks together, as suggested in Chapter 2, even at the expense of productivity.

3.The group can heighten the perceived value of being a member of the group in three ways:

These recommendations can help a group become more cohesive. The members of a highly cohesive group are well adapted to cooperate with one another and to compete with other groups. This ability to compete is an important aspect of cohesiveness. In the next chapter we will shift our attention from the dynamics within a group to the dynamics of conflict between groups.

II

Women participation in Sports:History

Women's participation in Sports

Women's sportsinclude amateur as well as Women professional sports in virtually all varieties of sports. Female participation in sports rose dramatically in the twentieth century, especially in the last quarter, reflecting changes in modern societies that emphasized gender parity. Although the level of participation and performance still varies greatly by country and by sport, Women's sports have broad acceptance throughout the world in the 2010s. In a few instances, such as figure skating, women athletes rival or exceed their male counterparts in popularity. An important aspect of women's sports is that women usually do not compete on equal terms against men.

Ancient civilizations

Before each ancient Olympic game, there was a separate women's athletic event, the Heraean games, dedicated to the goddess Hera and held at the same stadium at Olympia. Myth held that the Heraea was founded by Hippodameia the wife of the king who founded the Olympics.

Although married women were excluded from the Olympics even as spectators, cynical won an Olympic game as owner of a chariot (champions of chariot races were owners, not riders), as did Euryleonis, Belistiche, Zeuxo, Encrateia and Hermione, Timareta, Theodota, and Cassia. After the classical period, there was some participation by women in men's athletic festivals.

Early modern

During the song, yuan, and ming dynasties, women played in professional cuju teams. The first Olympic Games in the modern era, which were in 1896 were not open to women, but since then the number of women who have participated in the Olympic games has increased dramatically.

19th and early 20th centuries

The educational committees of the french revolution (1789) included intellectual, moral, and physical education for girls and boys alike. With the victory of Napoleon less than twenty years later, physical education was reduced to military preparedness for boys and men. In Germany, the physical education of Gutsmuths (1793) included girls' education. This included the measurement of the performances of girls. This led to women's sports being more actively pursued in Germany than in most other countries. When the federation sportive feminine International was formed as an all-women's international organization it had a German male vice-president and German international success in elite sports.

Women's sports in the late 1800s focused on correct posture, facial and bodily beauty, muscles, and health. In 1916 the Amateur Athletic Union (AAU) held its first national championship for women. Few women competed in sports in Europe and North America until the late nineteenth and early twentieth centuries, as social changes favored increased female participation in society as equals with men. Although women were technically permitted to participate in many sports, relatively few did. There was often disapproval of those who did.

Bicycling has done more to emancipate women than anything else in the world. Susan B.Antony said "I stand and rejoice every time I see a woman ride on a wheel. It gives women a feeling of freedom and self-reliance."

The modern Olympics had female competitors from 1900 onward, though women at first participated in considerably fewer events than men. Women first made their appearance in the Olympic Games in Paris in 1900. That year, 22 women competed in tennis, sailing, croquet, equestrian, and golf. As of the IOC-Congress in Paris 1914 a woman's medal had formally the same weight as a man's in the official medal table. This left the decisions about women's participation in the individual international sports federations. Concern over the physical strength and stamina of women led to the discouragement of female participation in more physically intensive sports, and in some cases led to less physically demanding female versions of male sports. Thus netball was developed out of basketball and Softball out of baseball.

In response to the lack of support for women's international sport, the federation sportive feminine internation was founded in France. This organization initiated the women's word games which attracted the participation of nearly 20 countries and were held four times between 1922 and 1934. The International Olympic committee began to incorporate greater participation of women at the Olympics in response. The number of Olympic women athletes increased over five-fold in the period, going from 65 at the 1920 summer Olympics to 331 at the 1936 summer Olympics.

Most early women's professional sports leagues foundered. This is often attributed to a lack of spectator support. Amateur competitions became the primary venue for women's sports. Throughout the mid-twentieth century, Communist countries dominated many Olympic sports, including women's sports, due to state-sponsored athletic programs that were technically regarded as an amateur. The legacy of these programs endured, as former Communist countries continue to produce many of the top female athletes. Germany and Scandinavia also developed strong women's athletic programs in this period.

Women's participation in Sports Events in past times

Societal inequalities and biases against women have been present in multiple fields of life. Although this is changing, women have in the past been excluded from political decision-making, religious rites and other social activities (and in some cases still are). This social bias has also had an impact in sports events. Historically (apart from a few rare exceptions), women had not been allowed to participate in main sports events and their role was usually limited to spectating.

Women at the Olympics

The international Olympic committee (IOC) promotes women in sports in an effort to increase participation in the games as well as recognition of the well-being of women and girls in sports at all levels of sports and different structures within sports. This is consistent with the Olympic charter which promotes equality within sports for men and women by including both genders in these competitions. The IOC as well as the International Federations (IFS) and National Olympic Committees (NOCs) have been committed to the mandates of this Olympic charter. Multiple measures have been taken toward increasing the participation of women at governing and administrative levels as well as training and education for women in sports and the supporting administrative structures. Since 1991, all new sports asking to be included in the Olympic program must feature women's events. The 2012 Olympic games in London were the first Olympics where every participating country included female athletes. They were also the first Olympics in which women competed in all sports in the program. Women have competed in the Olympics since 1900, following an all-male Games in 1896.

Leadership within the IOC

The IOC is committed to promoting women's participation in sports as part of their sports administration. An attempt was made to have women occupy at least 20% of the decision-making positions of the legislative bodies by the end of 2005, but the attempt failed. The objective of at least 10% by the end of 2000 however, was achieved. As of May 2014, 24 women are active IOC members, which is 22.6%. In 1990 the first woman, Flor Isava Fonseca, was elected to the Executive Board. The Vice President of the IOC from 1997-to 2001 was a woman, Anita DeFrantz. An increasing number of women are serving as chairpersons on IOC commissions. The NOCs are also making progress toward the objective with 11 NOCS headed by female presidents. IOC- Recognized Federations' executive boards are 26% women. Winter and Summer IFs boards are only 17% women.

IOC Women and Sport Commission

There has been additional work from the IOC Women and Sport Commission, commissioned in 2004, after starting as a working group in 1995. Women in Sport Commission advise the IOC President and Executive Board to ensure equality with consideration of women in sport in policymaking. The IOC has also done much work through programs developed to educate women in leadership roles toward success in administrative positions in NOCs and National Sports Federations. Furthermore, Olympic Solidarity programs assist NOC's participation in various ways, including a special Women and Sport assistance program. Every year the IOC awards the "Women and Sport" trophy to persons or organizations making a considerable contribution to women's sports.

Every four years the IOC conducts a world conference to review and plan actions to improve women's sports participation and promote gender equality in sports. A specific declaration was made at the 2012 conference in Los Angeles to collaborate and promote equality and use sport as a tool to improve women's lives (Olympic.org) The representation of women in the Olympics has always been below 50%. It has risen from about 10% until World War II to 44% in 2012. One cause of this is that some sports that have been historically popular with women are not included in the Olympics or have been included only recently.

Women's participation in the Summer Olympic Games

In the first modern Summer Olympic Games in 1896, only male athletes competed. Women had a secondary role during the re-birth of the Olympic movement, as the founder of the modern Games,

Pierre de Coubertin, envisioned an athletic event only for men. Athletic competitions were promoted as an outlet for men's physical strength and endurance while also forging their moral compass. Coubertin and his fellow organizers originally intended that women be only allowed to take part as spectators, not as athletes. They may have believed that women were neither strong nor competitive enough to participate in such an important sports event.

The situation changed quickly though; and while women missed the first games in 1896, they made their debut in the Summer Olympic Games of 1900. 22 women competed in the following two sports events: golf and tennis. In the next Games of 1904, women also competed in archery. Other sports were slowly added to the list, but the gap did not begin to close drastically until the 1980s. The first main sports federation that supported the participation and inclusion of women in competitions was the International Swimming Federation (ISF), which voted to include women in swimming at the Games of 1912. Their active involvement in women's sports prompted other international sports federations to begin including women in their competitions. Prior to the 1940s, women's athletic associations were informal and did not endorse competition. This changed after World War II and the number of female competitors rose. The graph below depicts women's participation in the Summer Olympic Games.

Attending the games

In some countries like Australia, getting funding for women to participate in the Olympics during the early years of the Games was difficult. Twenty years ago, the Australian swimming federation did not want to spend money to send female athletes to compete in the games; rather, they wanted to spend money to fund more participation of male swimmers. Sending a woman athlete (like Thelma kench from New Zealand in 1932) also required the extra cost of a chaperone with the team.

Media coverage

Historically, coverage and inclusion of women's team sports in the Olympics have been limited. Instead, the media focuses on female athletes in non-team competitions and on team sports played equally by both genders. NBC spends a smaller portion of coverage time on women than men in the Winter Olympics, but during the summer Olympics women seem to get a more equal share of attention. In the 2012 summer Games, NBC actually spent more time on women than men, and women received 55% of clock time within NBC's telecast at the London games. "If your primary concern is to see the US win medals, the last couple of Olympics, the women are winning the majority of the medals, you're going to be showing more women's sport," says Billings. When women's sports are covered in the media, that doesn't mean they are represented well by the commentators. There will generally be comments about how women's sports are years behind men's sports in what the athletes are able to accomplish. You also hear a lot about how a woman was lucky if she succeeded in a sport, rather than about her ability and commitment.

The women in non-contact or graceful, less aggressive sports, have been getting much more TV time. If you're a gymnast, diver, runner, swimmer, or volleyball player, you're more likely to be covered. If you compete in judo or shot-put, you're out of luck. Women's beach volleyball tends to get a lot of coverage, but there are arguments over why this is so. Although it is an awesome sport and America happens to have some of the best sand volleyball players there are, it is questionable if they receive more coverage because of their talent, or because of their outfits. In 2008, when all four American Olympic volleyball teams (beach and indoor, men's and women's) medaled, the women's beach volleyball team received more coverage than either men's team; the women's indoor team wasn't covered at all.

The Games: Sports

Since 1991, all new sports asking to be included in the Olympic program must feature women's events. The 2012 Olympic games in London were the first Olympics in which women competed in all sports in the program.

According to The International Olympic Committee's list of women's sports (updated in May 2014) were the following years every new woman's sport was introduced. The first women's sports were in 1900, which were tennis and golf. The next 3 Olympics added archery (1904), tennis and figure skating (1908), and swimming (1912). The next sports were not added until twelve-sixteen years later, fencing (1924) and gymnastics (1928). The second winter sport added to women's sports was alpine skiing in 1936. Another long twelve to sixteen years later, canoeing was added in 1948 and equestrian sports in 1952. Two Olympics followed, and speed skating was added to the games in 1960. In the following Olympics, volleyball and luge were added in 1964; rowing, basketball, and handball were added in 1976; field hockey was added in 1980; shooting and cycling were introduced in 1984. The next two Olympic terms included 6 more women's sports, tennis, table tennis, sailing in 1988, and badminton, judo, and biathlon in 1992. In 1996, football and softball; in 1998, curling and ice hockey; in 2000, weightlifting, pantheon, taekwondo, and triathlon, in 2002, bobsleighing was added; in 2004, wrestling; in 2008, BMX. The last updated women's sports included in the Olympic games according to the IOC are boxing (2012) and ski jumping (2014).

Basketball

Women's basketball has been contested in the Summer Olympics since 1976.

Boxing

It took over 100 years from when men's boxing

was announced for women's boxing to be announced. Women's boxing was first introduced at the 2012 summer Olympics with Nicola Adams winning the first boxing gold medal in the flyweight division.

Cycling

While men's road and track cycling have been Olympic disciplines since the first modern Olympics in Athens in 1896, there were no women's cycling events in the Olympic program until the

1984 games in Los Angeles when the first women's road race. The first track cycling event for women followed in 1988, but the 2012 London Games were the first with equal numbers of events for men and women, which entailed a reduction in the number of men's events as well as an increase in the number of women's events. The disciplines of mountain biking and BMX were introduced in 1996 and 2008 respectively, with separate men's and women's events from the outset.

Ice hockey

Canadian Hayley wickenheiser is the all-time leading scorer in the women's tournament and was named tournament MVP twice.

At the 99 IOC session in July 1992, the IOC voted to approve women's hockey as an Olympic event beginning with the 1998 winter Olympics as part of their effort to increase the number of female athletes at the Olympics. Women's hockey had not been in the program when Nagano, Japan had won the right to host the Olympics, and the decision required approval by the Nagano Winter Olympic Organizing Committee (NWOOC). The NWOOC was initially hesitant to include the event because of the additional costs of staging the tournament and because they felt their team, which had failed to qualify for that year's world championships.

could not be competitive. According to Glynis Peters, the Canadian Amateur Hockey Association (CAHA) head of female hockey, "the Japanese would have to finance an entirely new sports operation to bring their team up to Olympic standards in six years, which they were also really reluctant to do." In November 1992, the NWOOC and IOC Coordination Committee reached an agreement to include a women's ice hockey tournament in the program. Part of the agreement was that the tournament would be limited to six teams, and no additional facilities would be built. The CAHA also agreed to help build and train the Japanese team so that it could be more competitive. The IOC had agreed that if the NWOOC had not approved the event, it would be held at the 2002 winter Olympics. The format of the first tournament was similar to the men's: preliminary round-robin games followed by a medal-round playoff.

Softball

Softball at the summer Olympics In 1991, fast-pitch softballwas selected to debut as a medal event for women-only at the 1996 summer Olympics The 1996 Olympics also marked a key era in the introduction of technology in softball; the IOC funded a landmark biomechanical study on pitching during the games. The 117 meeting of the International Olympic Committee, held in Singapore in July 2005, voted to drop softball and baseball for the 2012 Summer Olympic games. Attempts to get softball readded to the Olympic program for the2016 games failed when the International Olympic Committee executive board instead selected golf and rugby sevens. The United States has won three of the four Olympics tournaments.

Weightlifting

Women's weightlifting made its Olympic debut at the 2000 Games in Sydney, with the following weight classes: 48 kg, 53 kg, 58 kg, 63 kg, 69 kg,75 kg, +75 kg

Women's sports

Throughout the history of the Olympics, sports popular exclusively with women or that have been very popular with women have been excluded. The situation extends beyond the popular women's sport of netball to women's cycling, which was excluded for many years despite having world championships for women being organized by 1958 It extends to the field of Hockey a sport included for men as early as 1908 but not competed by women until 1980. lawn bowls is a popular women's sport that has been included in the commonwealth games for many years but has not made the Olympic program. While primarily a sport for women, netball allows for mixed-gendered teams, but the Olympics do not allow mixed-gendered team sports.

The issues facing netball are part of a larger issue involving female participation in the Olympics. At the 1992 Summer Olympic Games in Barcelona, there were 159 sports for men to compete in, 86 sports for women, and 12 sports for both men and women. At the

2000 Summer Olympic games, there were still sports that women were excluded from participating in, such as boxing, wrestling, and baseball-softball was included as a women-only event. The issue of male over-representation in terms of a total number of sports and athletes is structural. In the United Kingdom, for example, more male athletes than female athletes received financial support. Sports officials rationalized this uneven distribution of funding by claiming that there are more opportunities for men to win on the highest level than there are comparable opportunities for women. The importance of netball being included as a competition sport in the Summer Olympics has been compared to softball and the benefits that the sport derived from Olympic inclusion. This included additional media attention and television coverage, especially during the Olympic years. Olympic recognition plays an important part in getting sponsorship for local competitions around the world. It also plays an important role in providing recognition to and opportunities for females that may not be available otherwise.

The selection of women's team's sport in the Olympics may not match with interest levels in a country. In Australia for example, 245,300 total women and girls play basketball, hockey, soccer, softball, and volleyball. This compares to 319,500 women and girls who play netball. Since 1991, all new sports asking to be included in the Olympic program must feature women's events. The 2012 Olympic games in London were the first Olympics in which women competed in all sports in the program.

Funding

The lack of Olympic recognition hampered the globalization of the game in developing countries because the Olympic Solidarity Movement provides access to funding for these nations through the International Olympic Committee. In some countries such as Tanzania, the lack of access to Olympic funding cut off other funding options such as funding by the British council. With official recognition, funding from the IOC, the Olympic Solidarity Movement, and the British Council became available to cover costs for travel to international competitions. For some nations, without that assistance, trying to maintain international caliber teams was difficult. Olympic recognition brought money to the development of the sport. In 2004, IFNA received a grant of US$10,000 from the IOC for development. IFNA was given an additional US$3,300 a year until 2007 by the Association of IOC Recognized International Sports (ARISF).

Beyond access to funds from the International Olympic Committee, Olympic recognition is often a requirement for getting funding from state and national sporting bodies and state and federal governments. This has been the case in Australia, and British Colombia. In 1985, the Australian sports commission and the official status of women identified five criteria for obtaining federal funding. One of these was: "status as an Olympic sport and its size by registrations In British Columbia, one of the guidelines says that in order to receive funding, "The sport must be on the program for either the 2011 or 2013 Canada Games and/or next to the scheduled recognized international multi-sport games (Olympics/ Paralympics, Pan American or Commonwealth Games, Special Olympic World Games). At the 2012 summer Olympics, the American team, for the first time, had more female athletes, 269, than male, 261.

Women sports in India

Women are the backbone of not only a family but the entire society. They are great achievers who play a major role in empowering society. The women not only in India but worldwide are underestimated and their capabilities are undermined in comparison to men yet they seek a way out to outshine men. They are mere watchers who are humiliated in different domains of the profession and are not allowed to pursue their dreams and career. Several women in sports in India have tried to break free from the shackles of discrimination, social deprivation, and cultural biases to establish a promising career for themselves.

Female athletes have occupied an esteemed place in society by acquiring numerous roles other than being just a mother. Their hard work and passion to prove themselves has helped them attain respect and they are finally acknowledged and appreciated. The mindset of people has revolutionized and they have started considering women as admirable beings who inspire the rest of the world to become the best. Perhaps, the phenomenal growth of women is a remarkable outcome of their dedication and desires.

A sport is a field that unites every person worldwide including women in sports. There are several phenomenal women athletes that are admired and have inspired the young generation to step forward and live their dreams. When it comes to sports for women, things are not very easy for them and they have to undergo hardships to rise above men. Even though men are more celebrated and paid higher in comparison to women yet female athletes seek their way out of all the challenges through their dedication and hard work

Women in sports industry have helped change the mindset of people in many ways.

Karnam Malleswari, Geeta Phogat, P.V.Sindhu, Mary Kom,Sakshi Malik,Saina Nehwal,Sania Mirza, Deepika Pallikal, Mithali Raj,Deepika Kumari,K Kansha Singh,Tanya Sachdeva,Chhanda Gayen,Sharmila Nicollet ,Kunjarani Devi are a few to name amongst many female sportsperson who helps you realize the change in area of sports

III
SOCIAL MEDIA IN SPORT

DEFINITION OF MEDIA

Media is the collective communication outlets or tools that are used to store and deliver information data. It is either associated with communication media or specialized mass media communication businesses such as and publishing. print media ,photography,adverising,cinema,broadcasting (ratio and television) and the press.

TYPES OF MEDIA

The term news media refers to the groups that communicate information and news to people. most Americans get their information about government from the news media because it would be impossible to gather all the news themselves. Media outlets have responded to the increasing reliance of Americans on television and the internet by making the news even more readily available to people. There are three main types of news media: print media, broadcast media, and the internet. Cohesion can be more specifically defined as the tendency for a group to be in unity while working towards a goal or to satisfy the emotional needs of its members. This definition includes important aspects of cohesiveness, including its multidimensionality, dynamic nature, instrumental basis, and emotional dimension. Its multidimensionality refers to how cohesion is based on many factors. This definition can be generalized to most groups characterized by the group definition discussed above. These groups include sports teams, workgroups, military units, fraternity groups, and social groups. However, it is important to note that other researchers claim that cohesion can not be generalized across many groups.

Characteristics Five characteristics of mass communication have been identified by Cambridge University's John Thompson. Comprises both technical and institutional methods of Production and distribution.

i) This is evident throughout the history of the media, from print to the internet, each suitable for commercial utility. Involves the com modification of symbolic forms, as the

ii) Production of materials relies on its ability to manufacture and sell large quantities of the work. Just as radio stations rely on its time sold to advertisements, newspapers rely for the same reasons on its space. Separate contexts between the production and reception· of information. Its reach to those "far removed" in time and space, in Comparison to the producers.

iii) Information distribution – a "one to many" form of Communication, whereby products are mass-produced and disseminated to a great quantity of audiences.

PRINT MEDIA

Theoldestmediaformsarenewspapers, magazines, journals, newsletters, and other printed material. These publications are collectively known as the print media. Although print media readership has declined in the last few decades, many Americans still read a newspaper every day or a news magazine onaregular basis. The influence of print media is therefore significant. Regular readers of print media tend to be more likely to be politically active.

The print media is responsible for more reporting than other news sources. Many news reports on television, for example are merely follow -up stories about news first appearedin newspaper, the top American news papers, such the new work times, the Washington post and Angeles Times, often set the agenda for many other media sources.

THE NEWS PAPER OF RECORD

Because of its history of excellence and influence,the NewYork Times is sometimes called the news paper of record: If a story is not in the Times, it is not important. In 2003, however, the newspaper suffered a major blow toitscredibilitywhenTimesjournalistJaysonBlairadmitted that he had fabricated some of his stories. TheTimes hassincemade extensive efforts to prevent any similar scandals, but some readers have lost trust in the paper.

BROADCAST MEDIA

Broadcast mediaare news reports broadcast via radio and television. Television news is hugely important in the United States because more Americans get their news from Angeles Times, often set the agenda for many other media sources.

TELEVISION NEWS

the main broadcast network-ABC, CBS and NBC each have a news division that broadcast sanightly newsshow for the fiftyyears most American swatched one or more of these broadcasts Since the1980s, however,cable news channels have chipped away at the broad cast net works many people who want to follow a story closely tune in to these stations first broadcasting news programs,The relatively new Fox network news program has also drawn numerous viewers away from the big three networks.

RADIO NEWS

The other type of broadcast media is radio. Before the advent of television in the 1950s, most American srelied on radio broadcasts for their news. Although fewer Americans rely on radio as their primary news source,many peoples tilllistentoradionewseveryday,especially during morning and evening commutes.Local news stations have a particularly large audience because they can report on local weather, traffic, and events.

TALK RADIO

Since the 1980s, talk radio has emerged as a major force in broadcasting.Talk radio is a radio formation which the hosts mixinterviews with political ommentary. A sa result,many talk radio show are highly partisan.Conservatives have a strong hold on American talk radio through program hosted by influential commentators, such as Rush Limbaugh and Sean Hannity.

THE INTERNET

The Internet is slowly transforming the news media because more American sarerelying on online sources of news instead of traditional print and broadcast media. Americans surf the sites of more traditional media outlets, such as NBC and CNN, but also turn to unique online news sources such as weblogs. Websites can provide text, audio, and video information, all of the ways traditional media are transmitted. The web also allows for more inter active approach by allowing people to personally tailor the news they receive via personalized web portals, newsgroups,podcas.

FUNCTIONS OF THE MEDIA

The media has immense power within the American democracy because just about all Americans get their news from the media rather than from other people or other sources.Mediac overa ges shape show Americans perceive the world and what they consider to be important. Voters and politician as like must pay attention to the media. In the American political system, the media perform number offunctionsimportanttothedemocratic process. The media reports the news, serves as an intermediary between the government and the people, helps determine which issues should be discussed, and keeps people actively involved in society and politics.

Reporting the News

Perhaps the most important role of the media in politics is to report the news. As noted above, the vast majority of people must trust the media to provide the with information. Democracy requires that citizens be informed because they must be able to make educated voting choices.

Media Bias

These days, politicians often complain of bias in the media,usually a liberal bias against the views of conservative politicians. They complain that the medias ability to decide which stories to report often reflects its partisanship. Although this is true to some extent, most major newspapers and television news stations report the same tories moreorless objectively. Biasis often restricted to the media outlet's commentary and opinion pages.

TYPES OF REPORTING

For much of American history (until the early twentieth century), most news media were clearly and open lybiased. Many newspapers,for example,were simply the voices of the political parties. This type ofjournalismiscalled partisan journalism. Othernewspaperspracticedyellowjournalism,reporting hocking and sordid stories in order to attract readers and sell more papers. Objective reporting (also called descriptive reporting) did not appear until the early twentieth century. News paper publishers such as Adolph Ochs of the New York Times championed objective journalism and praised reporters for simply reporting the facts. Although most journalists today still practice objective journalism, more and more are beginning to analyze and interpret the material they present, apracticecalled interpretive reporting.

YELLOW JOURNALISM

The media has influenced politics throughout American history. The most prominent and notorious example is the role of William Randolph Hearst's newspaper sin starting the Spanish-American Warin1898. According to the legend, Hearst's papers ran many stories chronicling the cruelty of Spanish colonial rule.When the American battleship Maineexploded under mysterious circumstances, Hearstseized the moment,alleging that he Spanish had destroyed the ship. Warsoon followed. Few media moguls have this much direct influence, but with media consolidation, some worry that the media has to omuch power.

BEING THE COMMON CARRIER

The media plays acommon-carrier role by providing alien of communication between the government and the people.This communication goe sbothways: The people learn about what the governmentis doing, and the government learns from the media what the publicis thinking.

PACK JOURNALISM

Criticsallege that journalists often copy one another without doing their own investigating. When one newspaper runs a story, for example, many others will run similar stories soon afterward.Critics refer to this tendencyas pack journalism.

Acting as the Public Representative

The media some time public representativeby holding government officials accountable on behalf of the people. Many people argue that the media are ill-equipped to play this role because the media does not face the same type of accountability that politicians face. Serving as the representative of the public, moreover,could   undermine   he media'sobjectivitybecausetheactofrepresentingthepeoplemightrequire reporter stotakea position on an issue.

THE ROLE OF THE MEDIA IN SPORTS DEVELOPMENT

INTRODUCTION

Media is playing an important role in both the construction and destruction of sporting structures and practices. The media has also helped in developing the new competitions, events and leagues. New sport forms have appeared and old ones have become of less importance. Of all the activities in the contemporary society that enjoy incredible development and massive followership, sports hold an eminent place. It is the submission of a significant multitude that the media and its continuous growth, are largely responsible for this achievement.

THE ROLE OF THE MEDIA

This makes sports attractive and lucrative.Little wonder too that sports command high followership. Surely, it is a perfect opportunity to invest and advertise,even in collaboration with the athletes themselves. It is therefore not strange that athletes from poor and illiterate background,become multi-billionaires.

Sport (or sports) in all forms of usually competitive physical activity which, through casual or organized participation, aim to use, maintain or improve physical ability and skills while providing entertainment to participants and in some cases, spectators either in teams or competing as individuals. Anyone can take part in sports. Sport is generally recognized as activities which are based in physical athleticism or physical dexterity. A number of competitive, but non-physical, activities claim recognition as mind sports. The International Olympic Committee (through ARISF) recognizes both chess and bridge as bonafide sports and Sport Accord, the international sports federation association, recognizes five non-physical sports although limits the amount of mind games which can be admitted as sports. Sports are usually governed by a set of rules or customs, which serve to ensure fair competition. Winning can be determined by physical events such as scoring goals or crossing a line first, or by the determination of judges who are scoring elements of the sporting performance, including objective or subjective measures such as technical performance or artistic impression. The media encourages people to develop reasonable interest sin engaging in sports.Either for fun,excitement, recreation, physical fitness or healthcare. In the homes, countless number of youths involve themselves in sporting activities. This has contributed to the remarkable improvement of fitness among the youths.

Many sports publicly condemn and penalize racism and similar forms of discrimination. Today, sports have been able to utilize the media in projecting the cause for child education. Governments of several countries have through the media, used sports to promote the education of children, and the need for young people to work harder toward as set goal.

THE ADVERSECIR CUMSTANCES OF THE MEDIA

Fanaticism in sports is no doubt a potential danger and a challenge that rocks today's society. There is no doubt too that the media contributes to fanaticism. The efficiency of the media in transmitting sports gives fans interrupted opportunities to support their teams. A pitiable number of fans are strangers to curtailing the excesses posed by sports; unending excesses which inmodern day is traced to the media. With such media excesses,sports fanatic and friends fallguilty of consciously orun consciously substituting sports for God. We had said that sports, with the aid of the media, are pivot alin the advance mentof the campaign for education.But the fashion in which the athletes are glamorously celebrated by the media campaign. Asstatedearlier,literacyis no criterion for being the best athlete in the world.And young people, fully cognizant of this, opt for sportsinplaceofeducation, as the quick estmeans to success and fame.

It is a fact that the media has been able to capture the attention of both the young and the old; and using sports as one of its attractions, many exhausts valuable time on sports. We stand to wonder what impact parents can make in guiding the young who are glued two four seven to their media devices from where they choose role models.

THE IMPORTANCE OF SOCIAL MEDIA IN SPORT

The Sport-Media Partnership Sports has become big business. It is now a well established global industry with International Olympic Committee. Sport, but not in all its forms, has something to sell. It has its events leagues, clubs and elite performers. Sports can make money but sportsmen get very little part of the earned money by different leagues. The relationship with media is central to the political economy of sport. Through media, we can get all type of information's about sports.

Mobile technologies and social media are transforming sports and sports businesses. Here, Andrew Cave andAlexMillercharta digital revolution More than half a million people converge on the Wimbledon Championships each year. While the focus is on the grasscourts, businesses traditionally seek to be nefit from hospitality,sponsorship and networking.

By engaging fans via social media, sports rights holders can open new communication channels with their audiencethatcanbemeasuredandvaluedasanewcommercialopportunity with sponsors.Businesses that get involved through sponsorships and social media promotions, mean while, benefit from increased brand affinity and loyalty.Yet sports clubs and businesses are only beginning to appreciate the potential that this offers. Barcelona has become the world's largest sports club on social media with followers expected to approach 150 million this year. Last year, it worked with sports marketing agency IMG to examine what value social media add stoitsshirtsponsorshiprights.Over one weekend.

"We found there was an extraordinary amount of value that the shirt sponsor of Barcelona was receiving on social media, which was n'treallyfactor edin to the sponsorship,"says RobMason,managing director of IMG Consulting, IMG's advisory, and brand strategy and activation division. Golf has also dived into social media and digital technology. "This has been the biggest sea change for all sports rights holders in the past few years," says MarkLichtenhein, the PGA European Tour's head of television,digital media and technology."Wenowhaveadialogue with the fan base. We never had that before. We were just a business-to-business industry selling our content to broad casters and rights to sponsors."

Thechallengeforbusinessesistofindwaysofmeasuring the value of social media denies Taylor, chief information officer for AEG, which owns the lease on theO2, says: "There is so much business potential. There are opportunities for revenue generation whether through ticketing platforms where we can offer upsells on tickets,or build products based on having more customer data.

The challenge for businesses is to find ways of measuring the value social media offers, beyond simple page views and unique user data. "Increasingly we are building social media benefits into sponsorship contracts butit's a mistake to measure it in a narrow vertical, "You have to look more holistically in terms of how it adds value to the brand, its audience reach. An investment in digital media may come back through other revenue streams. The more popular your product is, the better rights values you can attract."

The media involvement to the changing face of sport Today media, especially television offer sport added attractions in terms of finance from broadcasting fees and exposure to advertisers, sponsors and a wider audience. So, sports organizations are very keen to get involved with media. To some extent, media also has some degree control over sports organizations and sports.

PLAYING CATCH-UP

Interesting the seeds for articles get planted, but it does seem like everyone is in "catch up" clients, friends, colleagues, sometimes even strangers rushing by that they wish they could create more time in their day in order to get everything done that needs to get done well. Transmission of radio and television programmes from a radio or television station to home receivers is transmitted using a combination of satellite and wired transmission like cable television are also considered broadcasts and do not require a license. Transmissions of television and radio through digital technology have increasingly been referred to as broadcasting as well, during the past years, we have seen as increasing involvement of social media in sports.

Gender quality of Sports

Women and other non-binary genders have been at the receiving end of centuries of gender-based discrimination. While sports is one platform that leaves behind all the bars of caste, gender and race, there is stark gender discrimination visible. In most spheres, 'sport' has been glorified for its positive values like cooperation, mutual respect, equality and team spirit. Any discrimination based on gender or sexuality against athletes is against the very nature of any game.

While several national and international sporting platforms are focusing on hosting events of women and transgender people, local level competitions are still adamant about being gender-inclusive. For the Tokyo Olympics that recently concluded, 56 women athletes were representing the country. India is one of the countries that have profited the most from its surge in women athletes. The ability of sports to bring together people is not discussed enough in social circles Gender in sports has been a controversial issue ever since sports were invented. In the early years, sports were played only by the men, and the women were to sit on the sidelines and watch. This was another area of life exemplifying the sexism of people in which women were not allowed to do something that men could. However, over the last century in particular, things have begun to change

About As Book

The book Sociology in Physical Education is based on the revised curriculum of B.P.Ed. The Purpose of the book is to provide relevant text to the students. The book is written is simple language and easy to understand. The book will provide an authoritative source of information, not only for the students but also Sociologist, researchers. The book is written in simple language and easy to understand. I hope the book will not only useful for the students but also it helps Physical education teachers, researchers, Physical education professionals and coaches. They can enhance their knowledge on this subject with the help of this book. The importance and principles of Sociology in Physical Education, introductory level moderately difficult and challenging goals, relation of official and coach with management players and spectators, players versus spectators, recognizing yourself , measures of improving the standard of Sociology in Physical Education. Suggestions from the readers are always welcome to improve its future edition.